When U JUST CAN'T EVEN COPING WITH TRUMP

LOOK FOR OTHER MARIE RIVERS COLORING BOOKS:

FOLLOW MARIE RIVERS ON FACEBOOK!
WWW.FACEBOOK.COM/MARIERIVERSCOLORING

AND FIND MARIE RIVERS T-SHIRTS AT:
WWW.MARIERIVERS.THREADLESS.COM

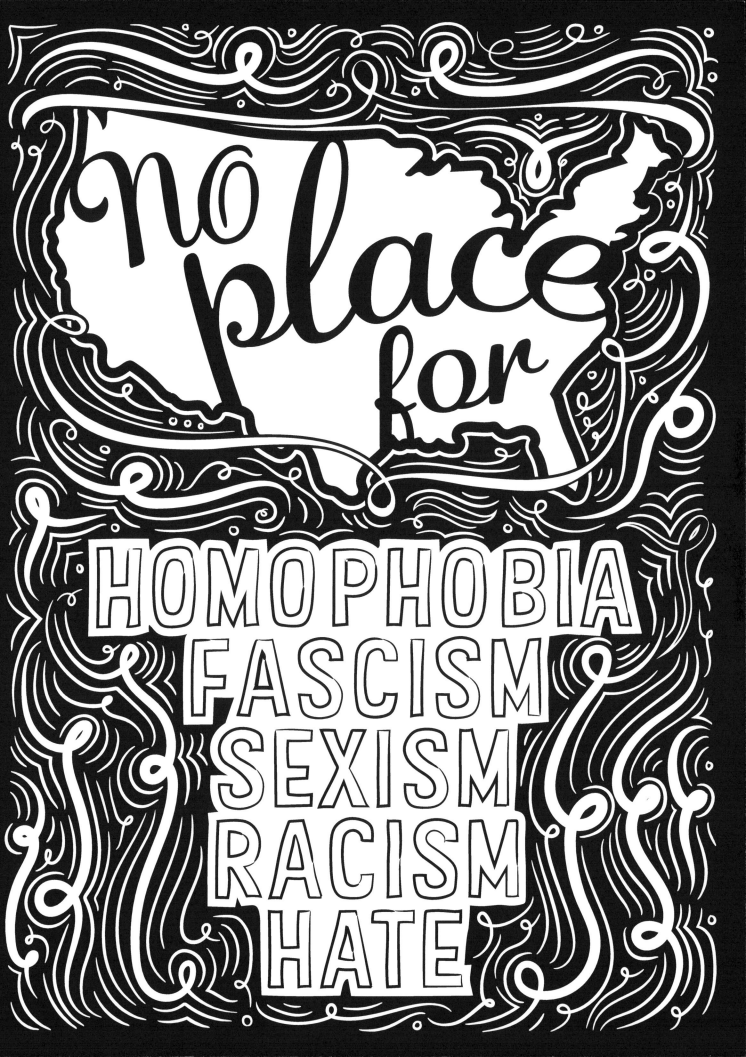

Made in United States
Troutdale, OR
11/21/2024